REVOLUTION!

THE FRENCH REVOLUTION

Adrian Gilbert

Wayland

REVOLUTION!

1848 Year of Revolution
The American Revolution
The Easter Rising
The French Revolution
Revolution in Europe 1989
The Russian Revolution

Cover picture: *Revolutionaries storm the Tuileries, the king's palace in Paris, and massacre the king's guard.*
Title page picture: *One of the enduring images of the French Revolution – an enemy of the people is led away to his execution, while the head of an earlier victim is carried above the crowd.*
Opposite: *A cockade, or rosette, worn like a badge on the hats of revolutionaries (see the banner on page 22). The words on this cockade mean 'Liberty! Equality!'.*

Book editor: Katrina Maitland Smith
Series editor: Paul Mason
Designer: Stonecastle Graphics Ltd

First published in 1995 by Wayland (Publishers) Ltd,
61 Western Road, Hove, East Sussex BN3 1JD, England

British Library Cataloguing in Publication Data
Gilbert, Adrian
French Revolution. - (Revolution! Series)
I. Title II. Series
944.04

ISBN 0 7502 1450 3

Typeset by Stonecastle Graphics Ltd, Marden, Tonbridge, Kent, England
Printed and bound by G. Canale & C.S.p.A., Turin, Italy

Picture Acknowledgements
The publishers would like to thank the following for permission to use their pictures in this book (t = top, b = bottom, l = left, r = right):
Archiv für Kunst und Geschichte (Berlin) title page, contents page, 5, 12 (both), 14, 15, 17 (tl), 18-19 (main picture), 20 (b), 22 (b), 26 (t), 26-7 (main picture), 28-9 (t), 30 (t), 31, 33, 34 (t), 36 (b), 37, 38 (t), 41, 42 (t), 43, 44, (London) 13; Bridgeman Art Library (Bibliotheque Nationale, Paris/ Giraudon) 4 (b), (Château de Versailles, France/Giraudon) cover, 7 (b), 23 (b), (Musée des Beaux-Arts, Lille/Giraudon) 35, (Musée de la Ville de Paris, Musée Carnavalet) 24, 36 (t), (Musée de la Ville de Paris, Musée Carnavalet/ Giraudon) 11, 16-17 (b), 18 (t), 39, 45 (b); Mary Evans Picture Library 10 (t), 30 (b), 32, 40, (Explorer) 4 (t), 6-7 (t); The Mansell Collection 17 (tr), 20 (t), 25, 28 (b), 38 (b); Peter Newark's Military Pictures 8; Wayland Picture Library 6 (b), 10 (b), 19 (r), 21, 22-3 (t), 34 (b), 45 (t).
Maps by Peter Bull.

CONTENTS

'THE KING IS DEAD – LONG LIVE THE REPUBLIC!'

King Louis XVI's last ride through the streets of Paris on 21 January 1793 was slow and quiet. Guarded by 1,200 troops from the National Guard, his coach took two hours to travel the short distance from his prison to the scaffold at the Place de la Révolution. The streets were lined with a silent crowd. They were eager to see blood, but they were in awe of the occasion. They were about to witness the violent death of their king.

In fact, Louis had been stripped of his crown four months earlier. His death sentence had been passed by the new revolutionary government, which disdainfully called him by his common name of Louis Capet. Louis had not been a popular ruler, but the calmness with which he prepared for death impressed all but the most fanatical of his opponents.

Above: *A prisoner of the revolutionaries, Louis is mocked by his guards. Hatred of the monarchy ran deep through much of France.*

THE KING'S LAST WORDS

From the scaffold, Louis looked around at the 20,000 upturned faces packed into the square. The former king spoke to the people in a firm voice: *'I die innocent of all the crimes of which I have been charged. I pardon those who have brought about my death, and I pray that the blood you are about to shed may never be required of France . . .'*[1] At that moment the officer in charge of the execution ordered a roll of drums, and Louis's final words were lost in the noise.

Louis stands on the scaffold to deliver his final speech to the crowd. The execution of Louis XVI shocked and outraged the crowned heads of Europe.

Left: *The head of Louis XVI is held aloft for the crowd to see; this was a traditional gesture to prove the death of the condemned man. Around the guillotine are ranks of soldiers, stationed there to ensure that the execution was carried out without interference, and to prevent any attempt to rescue Louis.*

After Louis had arrived at the place of execution, his jacket was removed and his hands tied behind his back. He climbed the ladder on to the scaffold. His hair was briskly cut by the Paris executioner, Sanson, leaving his neck bare for the guillotine's blade.

The Blade Falls

The former king was bound to the execution plank, face down, his head placed in the stocks between the upright posts of the guillotine. Executioner Sanson tugged the rope, and the heavy blade hurtled down. Louis's head fell into the waiting basket. One of Sanson's assistants picked it up and walked around the scaffold, displaying it to the crowd. Stunned, they were silent for a few moments, but then a great roar erupted, with shouts of *'Vive la Nation! Vive la République!'* Those in the front rushed forward to dip handkerchiefs and scraps of paper into the blood dripping down from the scaffold, to keep as souvenirs of this great event.

By killing the king, the revolutionaries demonstrated to the people of France (and the rest of the world) that they intended to break with the past. No longer would the nation be under the command of a king who claimed a divine right to rule. Instead, the people of France would rule themselves. Representatives would be elected by the people to form a government, and the government would do what the people wanted.

In the space of five years, the old way of running the country – known as the *ancien régime* – had been destroyed. The many privileges enjoyed by the king, his nobles and the clergy had been swept away. The changes were so important and dramatic that even at the time they were called a revolution.

Why had this revolution come about? The sudden and total collapse of the *ancien régime* was caused by deep social, economic and political problems that had built up to breaking point over a period of several decades. Even before the first signs of real protest erupted in 1789, France had travelled a long way down the road to revolution.

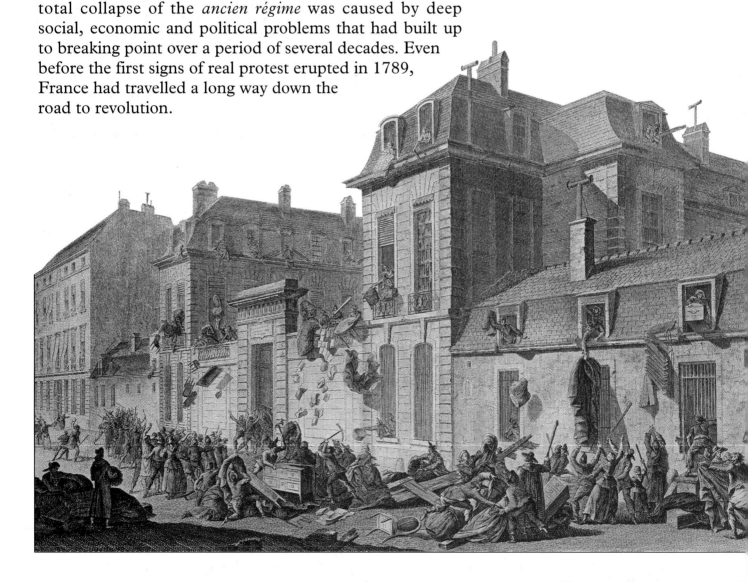

Above: *Women played an important part in mass demonstrations against the* ancien régime. *Here, the market women of Paris march on the king's palace at Versailles to demand cheap bread.*

Left: *The Hôtel de Castries is plundered. Parisians were short of food and eager to gain a share of the spoils. Outbursts of mob violence became a common feature of the revolution.*

Right: *Louis XVI, dressed in all the finery of his court robes. Although a well-meaning man, Louis had no idea of the seriousness of the situation facing France in 1789. Because he was unable to act forcefully to reform the French state, revolution became inevitable.*

LOUIS XVI (1754-93)

Louis was twenty years old when he was crowned King of France in 1774. Although he was a well-meaning man, he was not capable of leading a country in crisis. While he did his best to carry out his duties as a monarch, Louis preferred the simpler pleasures of a king's life, especially hunting. He rode in the great forests around the palace of Versailles almost every day. He was also a glutton. One observer noted that Louis once consumed for breakfast, *'four cutlets, a chicken, a plateful of ham, half a dozen eggs in sauce and a bottle and a half of champagne'.*

When the revolution began, Louis angered the more radical of the revolutionaries by repeatedly going back on his promises to accept important new reforms. His unpopularity increased through the actions of his wife, Marie Antoinette (1755-93). She was an Austrian princess whose extravagant lifestyle and total opposition to all reform made her many enemies amongst the people. Louis failed to understand that he would have to accept a new type of government. As a result, he first lost his crown and then his head.

THE ROAD TO REVOLUTION

In the 1780s, France was one of the great nations of Europe. Its population of twenty-six million was almost three times that of its nearest rival, Britain. France had recently engaged in a successful war against Britain, coming to the aid of the American colonists in the War of Independence (1775-83). Yet France's seemingly powerful position was weakened by serious problems.

The first great crisis was a desperate shortage of money. The French government had spent a fortune during the American War of Independence and, even in peacetime, its large army and navy continued to drain money away from the country. Vast sums had been borrowed by a series of finance ministers to keep the nation running. By the middle of the 1780s, however, it was clear that France was on the verge of bankruptcy.

The king and his ministers decided that government spending could not be cut back beyond an agreed limit. Thus the government would have to raise more money through increasing the taxes paid by the French people. This decision was to bring about a political crisis.

TIMELINE

1775-83
American War of Independence; with help from the French, American colonists defeat the British.

1786
French minister of finance, Charles Alexandre de Calonne, unsuccessfully attempts to introduce tax reforms.

1788
8 August: Decision taken to assemble the Estates General.

1789
April: Riots break out in Paris and the countryside.
5 May: Estates General assembles at Versailles.

The French navy defeats the British in a battle off the coast of Virginia, North America. The support given by the French government to the colonists in the American War of Independence drained France of money.

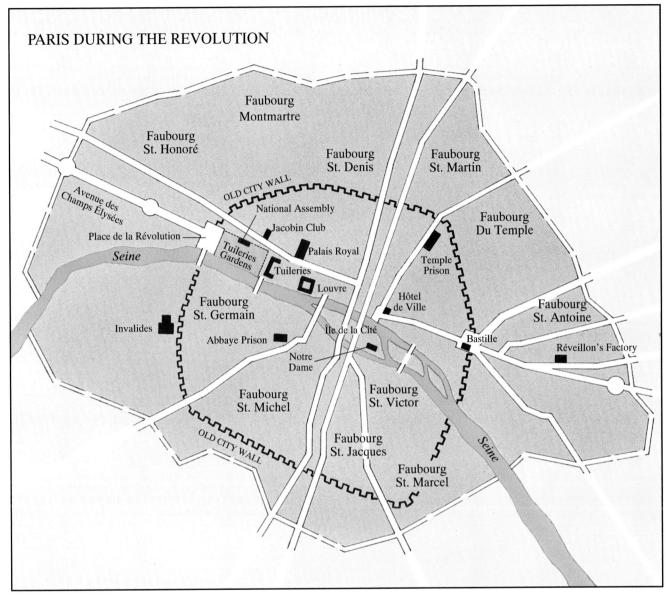

PARIS DURING THE REVOLUTION

Faubourg Montmartre

Faubourg St. Honoré

Faubourg St. Denis

Faubourg St. Martin

Avenue des Champs Élysées

OLD CITY WALL

National Assembly

Faubourg Du Temple

Jacobin Club

Place de la Révolution

Palais Royal

Seine

Tuileries Gardens

Temple Prison

Tuileries

Louvre

Faubourg St. Germain

Hôtel de Ville

Faubourg St. Antoine

Invalides

Île de la Cité

Bastille

Abbaye Prison

Réveillon's Factory

Notre Dame

Faubourg St. Michel

Faubourg St. Victor

OLD CITY WALL

Faubourg St. Jacques

Seine

Faubourg St. Marcel

Although no country in Europe in the 1780s operated a method of raising taxes that could be called fair by today's standards, the French system was particularly unjust. The people of France were divided into three groups or estates (see box, page 11), but the main burden of taxation fell upon only one group, the Third Estate. The more far-sighted of Louis XVI's ministers realized that they must extend taxation to the other two estates. This would bring in more money, and it would help stem the rising discontent felt by the Third Estate, which – not surprisingly – was beginning to protest at the government's constant demands for money from the Third Estate only.

Paris at the time of the French Revolution. Although revolution spread across the country, Paris remained at the centre of the uprising against royal rule. Many of the great events of the period took place within the boundaries of the old city wall. (The Faubourgs are districts of Paris.)

Noble Selfishness

In theory, it was an easy step for the king and his ministers to extend taxation to the other estates. Louis XVI was, like his predecessors, an 'absolute' monarch; he believed that he ruled through God's will, and that he had complete authority over his subjects. In practice this was not the case. Over a long period of time, the nobles had gained many privileges, which they would not give up – even for the king and the good of the country.

The French government tried to limit the powers of the nobles, but it had little success. This was partly due to Louis's weak personality. Although he knew that reform was vital if France was not to collapse, he did not have the strength of will to force through unpopular measures.

To add to the government's financial problems, the country was suffering from a worsening economic situation. As well as a general depression in trade and industry, there were bad harvests throughout the 1770s and 1780s. The prices of many essential foods – especially bread – went up, while people's wages went down.

Above: *The French minister of finance, Charles Alexandre de Calonne, saw the need for change.*

Below: *In 1787, to gain wider support for his reforms, Calonne asked the king to call an Assembly of Notables. This was a gathering of nobles chosen by the king to discuss affairs of state. Despite hopes that an agreement would be reached, the Assembly rejected Calonne's proposals.*

THE THREE ESTATES

The people of France were divided into three groups, called estates. The First Estate comprised the clergy, which was responsible for the country's spiritual and moral welfare, as well as the education of its children. Though the First Estate was a major landowner, it did not have to pay taxes on the land – it did, however, send a small amount of money to the government each year. Alongside bishops living in luxury, the clergy also included large numbers of poor parish priests who worked amongst the people. Of these, many were prepared to accept that change was needed.

The Second Estate, or nobility, paid very few taxes. It also had many other privileges, ranging from hunting rights over peasant lands to the

This cartoon shows a poor peasant of the Third Estate carrying the heavy burden of the other two estates of the clergy and nobility.

choice of the top jobs in the government and the army. A few nobles were keen to reform the system, but most were not prepared to give up their rights. Indeed, some were attempting to gain greater power for themselves at the expense of the king and his government.

Everyone else was lumped into the Third Estate. This included the vast majority of the people, ranging from the poorest to peasant farmers to lawyers and rich businessmen. The poorer people of the Third Estate wanted economic security through lower food prices. The better-off wanted a greater say in how the country was run, and to have a chance of getting the jobs traditionally reserved for the nobility. Whatever their background, the people of the Third Estate were agreed on one thing: that great change must come, and soon.

The misery and insecurity caused by the economic crisis spread to the fairly well-off peasant farmers and artisans, as well as the poor. This situation encouraged social discontent. By the spring of 1789 rioting had broken out across the country, and had become so serious that the army was placed on permanent standby to prevent violent protests from getting out of hand.

Onward to Versailles

With the country on the verge of breakdown, the government made one last attempt to sort out the mess. It decided to call the Estates General, a meeting of the representatives of the three estates, to discuss the country's difficulties and to restore order. The Estates General, which had not met since 1614, was to gather at Versailles, the king's palace just outside Paris. Each estate had very different views as to what should be the result of this great meeting.

Below: *The three estates formally make their way into the king's palace at Versailles on 5 May 1789 for the meeting of the Estates General.*

Left: *French troops charge down a demonstration by paper workers outside the Réveillon factory in Paris on 18 April 1789. The monarchy had always used the army to protect its position; increasingly, however, the army was not to be relied upon.*

Before the Estates General began its first session on 5 May 1789, each estate drew up lists of grievances and proposals called *cahiers de doléances*. As they made their way to Versailles with their *cahiers*, most of the representatives knew that some sort of change was inevitable. No one, however, could have had any idea that these proposals would lead to a full-scale revolution.

SALONS AND PHILOSOPHERS

During the eighteenth century, France experienced a transformation in the way people thought about how each person should be able to live within society. Philosophers and other intellectuals gathered in the houses of the wealthy to discuss the individual's rights and responsibilities, and how the country should be governed. Such meetings became known as salons, after the French name for the grand reception rooms in which they were held.

This movement, which was known as the Enlightenment, stressed the importance of reason over tradition. The Enlightenment philosophers argued that people should not obey the laws made by the government simply because they were told to do so. Instead, they should accept laws only if they believed that those laws were fair and reasonable.

This philosophy went against the teachings of the Church, as well as questioning the divine right of the king to rule, and had a great influence on many of the future leaders of the French Revolution. They now began to question the whole political system: maybe they should get rid of the king and develop a new system of government that was based on the will of the people.

This painting of a salon gathering includes the mathematician Jean le Rond d'Alembert, the writer Denis Diderot, and the composer Jean Philippe Rameau.

CITIZENS AND THE KING

Louis XVI addressed the three estates of France gathered at Versailles in May 1789. To the dismay of the Third Estate, he failed to give assurances that he was prepared to accept change. Dismay turned to anger when the nobility blocked any attempts by the Third Estate to introduce reform.

The leaders of the Third Estate decided to turn their backs on the nobles and clergy and, on 17 June, they adopted the title of the National Assembly. This was a direct challenge to royal authority, especially as they encouraged members from the other two estates to join them as equals.

The opening of the Estates General at Versailles on 5 May 1789. The king is visible at the back of the hall, sitting on his throne. Seated on Louis's right are the ranks of the clergy, with the nobility on his left. Directly facing him are the representatives of the Third Estate. In his opening address, Louis did not respond to the Third Estate's call for reform.

TIMELINE

1789

17 June: The Third Estate takes on the title of the National Assembly.

14 July: Fall of the Bastille.

26 August: 'Declaration of the Rights of Man and the Citizen'.

5-6 October: March of the market women; the Royal family and National Assembly are removed to Paris.

1790

13 February: Suppression of religious orders (except those engaged in teaching or charitable work).

19 June: Abolition of the titles of hereditary nobility.

12 July: The 'Civil Constitution of the Clergy' is published.

26 October: The king authorizes approaching foreign countries for possible help against the revolution.

1791

10 March: The 'Civil Constitution of the Clergy' is condemned by the Pope, the head of the Roman Catholic Church.

2 April: The Comte de Mirabeau dies following a short illness.

20 June: The 'flight to Varennes'; the king is brought back to Paris five days later.

1792

20 April: War is declared against Austria (and then Prussia).

11 July: France is officially proclaimed to be 'in danger' as enemy troops prepare to invade the country.

10 August: The Tuileries is stormed and the king is imprisoned and suspended from his official functions. The monarchy is effectively over.

Among those nobles who joined the National Assembly were the Comte de Mirabeau (1749-91) and the Marquis de Lafayette (1757-1834). Mirabeau was a hulking brute of a man, his face scarred by childhood smallpox; he dominated the speeches in the National Assembly with his powerful voice and skilful oratory. Determined to protect the Assembly, he also did his best to limit the revolution, so that there would still be a place for the king in the government of France. His death in 1791 robbed the revolution of one of the most influential voices for moderation. Lafayette, another moderate revolutionary, had led French forces during the American War of Independence. Personally ambitious, yet lacking real political awareness, Lafayette's reputation as a soldier and a patriot was welcomed by the Assembly.

Honoré Gabriel Riqueti, the Comte de Mirabeau, became one of the most effective of the early leaders of the French Revolution.

The day after the formation of the National Assembly, the members turned up to their usual meeting hall but found it locked and guarded by royal troops. Outraged by what they saw as an attempt to suppress the National Assembly, the members marched off to a nearby covered tennis court. There they swore 'never to separate' until a fair and proper form of government had been established.

The king and the majority of the nobility were horrified by the very idea of a National Assembly. However, they lacked the authority to oppose the challenge thrown down by the Third Estate. During June and early July of 1789, Louis reluctantly accepted the National Assembly. All the while, however, he was secretly ordering his troops to march on Versailles, where the Assembly gathered, to deal with these upstarts from the Third Estate.

Right: *The radical journalist Camille Desmoulins was influential in encouraging the people to take direct action. Waving two pistols aloft at the Palais Royal (far right), he calls to the crowd to arm themselves and defend the revolution. This demonstration of 12 July 1789 was a prelude to the march on the Bastille.*

Below: *The Tennis Court Oath was one of the great dramatic moments of the revolution, encouraging and strengthening the resolve of the newly formed National Assembly.*

Fear and Loathing

The king's attempt to restore order was prevented by events outside Paris. The unrest in the countryside increased through the summer of 1789. It reached fever pitch as large sections of the rural poor became convinced that the king and the nobles were deliberately hoarding grain. This was not the case at all but, in the minds of the poor, food shortages became part of a giant plot to starve them into submission. Called the 'Great Fear', this feeling of paranoia swept through the country. At its most extreme, the châteaux of rich landowners were broken into and their contents pillaged by the people. In almost all areas, the authority of the king's government collapsed. People from all classes now turned to the National Assembly for guidance.

Unrest began to affect the army, where morale and discipline had already been poor for many months previously. Soldiers were experiencing the same hardships as the rest of the people, and were no longer obeying orders. People sensed that the old order was beginning to break down. Meanwhile in Paris, a young lawyer-turned-journalist called Camille Desmoulins (1760-94) attracted large audiences with his attacks on the monarchy. He warned the people of the dangers to the revolution from the king, encouraging them to seize weapons to defend themselves against royal control.

On 12 July, brandishing two pistols, Desmoulins declared that he would never be taken alive by the king's agents (who followed him everywhere). Following this resounding call to arms, the crowd set off in search of muskets and ammunition.

On 14 July 1789, the people began to march on the prison-fortress of the Bastille, where the government held a store of arms and ammunition. To the ordinary people of Paris the Bastille was a symbol of all that was bad about the royal government. Its high walls dominated the poorer areas of the city, and in the past many unfortunate citizens had been flung into its dark dungeons. A great crowd gathered outside the Bastille, determined both to get rid of this hated symbol and seize the weapons housed in the prison. The Bastille's defenders comprised a few very nervous soldiers and, when one discharged a musket into the crowd, enraged Parisians surged forward, smashing down the gates and killing the prison's governor.

Two days after the fall of the Bastille, the minister of war informed Louis that the army could not be relied upon to support the monarchy. This was a crucial moment in the revolution. The king and the aristocracy were unable to use force to crush the revolution, the traditional response of the monarchy when dealing with social unrest. Instead, the king would have to come to some sort of agreement with the Assembly. While the Assembly wanted to preserve the monarchy – although with reduced power – the king and his followers only accepted compromise when it was forced upon them. This angered the Assembly, which became increasingly suspicious of the king's motives. Exasperated by the attitude of the king and his court, the Comte de Mirabeau exclaimed, *'I am a mad dog, from whose bites despotism and privilege will die.'* [2]

Left: *Revolutionaries break into the Invalides, a military home and warehouse, to gain arms and ammunition. Although ten cannon and 28,000 muskets were seized, the revolutionaries found little ammunition. This led to calls to storm the Bastille, which was said to contain a large store of gunpowder.*

Below: *A watercolour from the period shows the assault on the Bastille, on 14 July 1789. An old medieval fortress, the Bastille could have held out for some time, but the defenders were few in number and were poorly trained.*

TO THE BASTILLE!

Jean Baptiste Humbert, a Parisian watchmaker, was caught up in the events of 14 July, 1789: *'I was halted by a citizen, who informed me of shot being issued at the Hôtel de Ville. So I hastened there and was handed a few buckshot pellets. I then proceeded to the Bastille, loading as I went. I was joined by a group also on its way to the Bastille. We found four infantry of the Watch, armed with guns, and I begged them to join us. They replied that they lacked powder and shot. So we joined in giving each enough for two shots. Thus armed, they were glad to accompany us. As we passed before the Hôtel de Régie we observed that two cases of bullets had been smashed and bullets were being freely dispersed. I filled one of my pockets to give some to anyone who was short.'* [3]

Above: *After the fall of the Bastille, the Parisian mob set upon those they believed were making money by raising food prices. One of the accused, Foullon de Doué, was hanged from a lamppost on 23 July.*

Towards a New Government

Ignoring the king, the Assembly set about trying to organize a government. This was not an easy task as the country remained in a state of turmoil. So too did the Assembly, where passionate arguments and unruly behaviour made it difficult to form and pass new laws and resolutions. The actions of the Assembly caused Mirabeau to compare it to *the spectacle of young schoolboys escaped from the rod and mad with joy because they are promised an extra day's holiday.* [4]

The first serious step made by the Assembly was the abolition of the old feudal system on 4 August 1789. This was swiftly followed by the 'Declaration of the Rights of Man and the Citizen', a document setting out the basic principles of the new government. In order to provide a military force to back up the Assembly's laws, the Paris city militia was re-formed as the National Guard, under the leadership of Lafayette.

Yet the Assembly, for all its fine words, was unable to solve the country's economic problems which, if anything, got worse during the autumn of 1789. In Paris, bread shortages continued and rioting became commonplace. Many people blamed the king for these problems, and the radical members of the Assembly encouraged the people in their anti-royal sentiments.

Above: *The opening page of the new constitution, which contained the 'Declaration of the Rights of Man and the Citizen'.*

Below: *Men of the newly formed National Guard parade to the admiring glances of the men and women of Paris.*

THE STATE, THE CHURCH AND CASH

As the new government of France, the National Assembly had to find money to run the country. The breakdown in the taxation system – which had been made worse by the vast debts run up before the revolution – forced the Assembly to look for new ways of raising money. One obvious source was the Church, and its vast lands were taken over by the state and sold off to raise money.

Although there was opposition to this take-over by some members of the Church, many of the clergy supported a fairer distribution of its wealth. Other proposals by the Assembly were to cause greater problems. The main source of disagreement was the Assembly's reform called the 'Civil Constitution of the Clergy'. Issued in July 1790, it placed the Church under the direct authority of the government: members of the clergy would be elected by local assemblies and they would swear their allegiance to the state.

This was too much for many priests, who believed that the Church and the government should be separate. Pope Pius VI condemned the reforms in March 1791, and large numbers of the clergy refused to accept the state's authority in religious matters. They were often supported by the local community – indeed, the reforms caused many people, especially in rural areas, to oppose the revolution.

An anti-revolutionary print shows the mob running riot through a church. Violent attacks upon churches were not common, but they caused widespread unease about the way the revolution was being run.

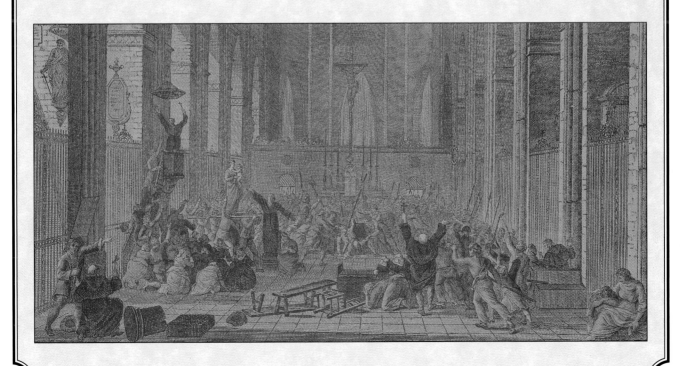

On 5 October, events boiled over and a mob of half-starved Parisians, led by the market women of the city, marched on Versailles. Once there, they confronted the king, demanding cheap food. Others insisted that the royal family be brought back to Paris, where they could be better controlled by the people. Fearing bloodshed, the king accepted the mob's demands, and he and his family left Versailles for the Tuileries palace in the capital.

Even while in Paris the king tried to stop the progress of the revolution. Louis had sent letters to the Emperor of Austria and other foreign leaders, calling for help to restore him to power. He was supported by many nobles, some of whom had left France in order to organize armed forces to invade the country from outside. Such people became known as *émigrés*.

The Onset of War

Relations between revolutionary France and the other major nations of Europe became steadily worse. The rulers of Austria and Prussia were horrified by events in France, fearful that revolution might break out in their own countries. A number of the French revolutionaries were actively encouraging the spread of revolution abroad, and war became inevitable. Yet the onset of war made the revolutionaries more determined than ever.

As foreign armies began to march into France in the summer of 1792, popular hostility to the king exploded. On 10 August, a mob invaded the Tuileries, massacred the king's Swiss Guard, and dragged the royal family to a prison called the Temple. The king's rule was suspended by the Assembly.

The first phase of the revolution was over. The attempt by the moderate revolutionaries to develop a system by which the king ruled with his people had failed. Now it was the turn of the radicals to take over. No longer would the French be subjects of the king; instead, they were to be citizens in a new republic.

Above and below: *In June 1791, Louis and his family tried to flee the country and join the* émigrés. *After a long chase, however, they were caught at the town of Varennes and brought back to Paris. A banner celebrating the capture (below) was presented to the people of Varennes. The red Phrygian cap at its centre was used by the revolutionaries as a symbol of liberty.*

Right: *A graphic depiction of the storming of the Tuileries. The soldiers in red coats are the Swiss Guard, whose unwavering loyalty to Louis caused particular anger amongst the mob.*

MASSACRE AT THE TULERIES

One of the last military units loyal to Louis XVI, the Swiss Guard fought determinedly to defend the king. A witness described how the guards were singled out by the enraged revolutionaries: *'The mob, master of the Palace's grand staircase, now overwhelms the interior. Swiftly it floods all the rooms and despatches all Swiss Guards in them. Corridors, roofs, offices, private exits, to the smallest wardrobes are searched, and any unfortunates hiding there are butchered without pity. Others are thrown alive from high windows, vainly beseeching mercy, and are transfixed by the pikes thrust from the terrace and courtyard.'* [5]

THE NEW REPUBLIC

The suspension of the king's powers in August 1792 did nothing to solve the desperate situation facing the revolutionaries. A large Prussian army had crossed the French border, captured the fortress town of Verdun and was bearing down upon Paris. The Prussian commander, the Duke of Brunswick, had issued a manifesto promising the full restoration of the French monarchy, and severe punishment for the leaders of the revolution.

The revolutionary French government, encouraged by the new minister of justice, the formidable Georges Jacques Danton, rallied its troops and rushed all available men to the front. Like Mirabeau, Danton was a large, ugly man but, as well as being a powerful orator, he was also an able organizer, which made him doubly effective in times of crisis. Trying to get the government to act decisively, Danton aptly summed up the situation: *'All this talk is meaningless. I see only the enemy.'* [6]

In Paris, panic swept the streets, deliberately encouraged by those extremists eager to push the revolution on to an ever more radical course. Pamphlets and newspapers were circulated, demanding that the most extreme measures should be taken against any French citizens opposing the revolution. Such views were fuelled by the desertion of Lafayette to the enemy side on 17 August, disillusioned at the radical course taken by the revolution.

Chief amongst those calling for death to all counter-revolutionaries was a journalist called Jean Paul Marat (1743-93). In the paper, *L'Ami du peuple* (or *The People's Friend*), Marat raged: *'Let the blood of these traitors flow. That is the only way to save the country.'* [7]

Massacre of the Innocents

Marat's words were taken literally by some extremists, who turned on the prisoners packed into the many gaols of Paris. Poorly guarded, the prisons were an easy target. In what became known as the September Massacres, around 1,200 prisoners were butchered in their cells. Their murderers justified their actions by claiming that the prisoners were plotting to overthrow the government.

Above: *Jean Paul Marat, one of the most extreme of the revolutionaries. He used his newspaper,* L'Ami du peuple, *to encourage the people to take violent action against the old order.*

Right: *A contemporary illustration depicting the killing of prisoners in the Abbaye. The September Massacres were a great explosion of barbarity, as the Parisian mob went on the rampage. Many innocent men and women were tortured, then murdered.*

THE SEPTEMBER MASSACRES

At the Abbaye prison, Jourgniac de Saint-Méard made this moving record of the prisoners as they waited for their fate: *'The most important matter that employed our thoughts was to consider what posture to adopt when we were dragged to the place of slaughter, in order to suffer death with the least pain. Occasionally we asked some of our companions to go to the window to watch the attitude of the victims. They came back to say that those who tried to protect themselves with their hands suffered the longest, because the blows of the knives were thus weakened before reaching the head; that some of the victims actually lost their hands and arms before their bodies fell; and that those who put their hands behind their backs obviously suffered less pain. We, therefore, recognized the advantage of this last posture and advised each other to adopt it when it came to our turn to be butchered.'* [8]

TIMELINE

1792
2–6 September: Massacre of prisoners in Paris.
20 September: French defeat Prussian army at Valmy; setting up of the Convention.
6 November: Austrians defeated by French at battle of Jemappes; French troops advance deeper into Belgium.

1793
21 January: Execution of Louis XVI.
1 February: France declares war on Britain and Holland.
11 March: Revolt in the Vendée begins.
18 March: French defeated at battle of Neerwinden in the Netherlands.
4 April: General Dumouriez deserts to the Austrians.
May–October: Federalist revolts in the provinces.
29 May–2 June: Fall of the Girondins.
13 July: Marat murdered by Charlotte Corday, a supporter of the deposed Girondins.

Most of the victims, however, were either clergy who refused to accept the Civil Constitution or minor criminals awaiting trial. Although this episode did not last long, it demonstrated the degree of hatred and violence that had been released by the revolution.

In the event, the Prussian army was defeated by the French at the battle of Valmy on 20 September 1792, and the military crisis was averted. Further French victories followed during the autumn of 1792, pushing the border of France eastward into Belgium.

The revolutionary leaders formed a new government on 20 September, called the Convention. The Convention immediately confirmed the abolition of the monarchy and, on 22 September, decreed that this date was to mark the beginning of Year One of the new French Republic. The Convention was more radical than the Assembly. It encouraged the spread of revolution to other countries and, after a short trial, sentenced the king to death.

Above: *A sheet of signatures made by French volunteers joining the battle against the Austrian and Prussian invaders of revolutionary France.*

Right: *France was soon at war with other European powers. At times, it seemed that France would fall to its enemies, but the superior military skill and determination of the French armies led eventually to a spectacular series of victories.*

Below: *A dramatic moment during the battle of Valmy, on 20 September 1792. Unable to break the French line, the Prussians retreated, and revolutionary France was saved from almost certain defeat.*

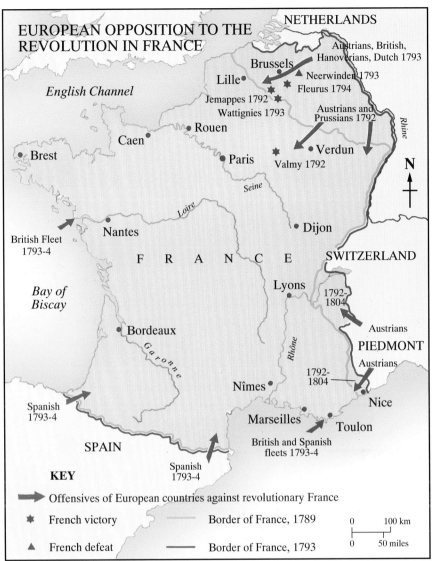

EUROPEAN OPPOSITION TO THE REVOLUTION IN FRANCE

NETHERLANDS

Austrians, British, Hanoverians, Dutch 1793

Brussels

Lille

Neerwinden 1793

Fleurus 1794

Jemappes 1792

Wattignies 1793

Austrians and Prussians 1792

English Channel

Rhine

Rouen

Caen

Brest

Paris

Verdun

Valmy 1792

N

Seine

Loire

Nantes

British Fleet 1793-4

Dijon

F   R   A   N   C   E

SWITZERLAND

Bay of Biscay

Lyons

1792-1804

Austrians

PIEDMONT

Bordeaux

Garonne

Rhône

1792-1804

Austrians

Nice

Nîmes

Marseilles

Toulon

Spanish 1793-4

British and Spanish fleets 1793-4

SPAIN

Spanish 1793-4

KEY

→ Offensives of European countries against revolutionary France

★ French victory   —— Border of France, 1789

▲ French defeat   —— Border of France, 1793

0   100 km

0   50 miles

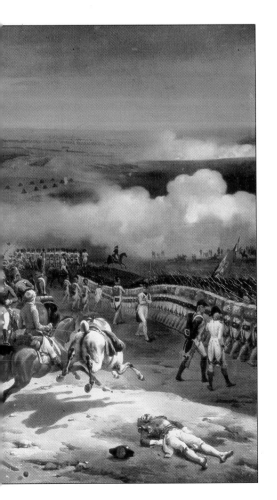

Louis's execution was dramatic evidence to the rest of Europe of the revolutionary intentions of the Convention and, by February 1793, France was at war with Britain and Holland. Danton challenged the foreign powers to do their worst: *'The kings in alliance try to intimidate us. We hurl at their feet, as a gage of battle, the French king's head.'* [9]

Within the Convention, several loose political groupings evolved, based around the political clubs and societies that had sprung up since the start of the revolution. Political fighting came to be concentrated in a struggle between the more moderate Girondins and the radical Jacobins (which included Danton and a new rising star in the revolution, Maximilien Robespierre).

In the contest between the two factions, the Jacobins were the more skilful. They looked beyond the debating chamber of the Convention to draw in the popular masses of Paris on their side. Increasingly politically active, the masses – especially the radical *sans-culottes* – were able to influence the decision-making of the Convention through rowdy street demonstrations and by the threat of violence – a new and decisive element of political life in Paris.

Enemies of the State

Émigré nobles were constantly plotting to overthrow the revolution, encouraging revolts within the country and working with foreign powers to invade France from outside. The uprising in the Vendée region in the west of France was the most serious of the royalist counter-revolutionary revolts. *Émigré* French troops were shipped by the British into the Vendée to support and encourage groups of local

GEORGES JACQUES DANTON (1759-94)

Like most of the leaders of the revolution, Danton came from a comfortable middle-class background. He trained as a lawyer, and was working in Paris when the Estates General was called in 1789. Danton threw himself into revolutionary activity and was an early member of the Jacobin Club. Although not immediately prominent in revolutionary politics, his radical zeal, enormous energy and great skill as an orator brought him political success.

Danton became minister of justice in the Convention, but he was also the guiding force in organizing the country to repel the foreign invasions in the spring and summer of 1792. A key voice in the call for the execution of the king and in the destruction of the moderate Girondin faction, Danton nevertheless became sickened by the later violent excesses of the revolution. His moderation brought him into conflict with Robespierre who, by early 1794, had gained power in the Convention. Danton was denounced and he and his followers were arrested and sent to the guillotine.

Georges Jacques Danton, one of the great leaders of the revolution. Initially a loyal Jacobin, his later call for moderation brought him into fatal conflict with Robespierre.

FRENCH RESISTANCE TO THE REVOLUTION

Above: *Making good use of the rough terrain, royalist supporters set up a concealed camp in the Vendée. Relying on aid from émigrés and from Britain, the royalists were able to maintain a long campaign.*

Right: *The revolutionaries' control over France was not complete until the end of 1793. Previously, the country had experienced repeated bouts of resistance both by federalists and royalists.*

KEY

Main areas of French resistance 1793-99

Resistance of Belgian peasants, 1798

Border of France, 1789

Border of France, 1799

people opposed to the revolution. The royalists achieved a number of early successes but argued amongst themselves and did not press home their advantage.

Elsewhere, opposition to the central government in Paris took the form of a series of federalist revolts. The federalists wanted greater local freedom and, in several areas of France, especially in the south, they achieved temporary success in expelling the revolutionaries from their towns and villages.

In the end, both the federalist and royalist revolts were put down by troops from the Convention, but the military situation on the borders had deteriorated. The Austrian army defeated the French at the battle of Neerwinden in the Netherlands, and the leading French commander, General Dumouriez, deserted to the enemy. The combination of military defeat and counter-revolution during the spring and summer of 1793 created a surge of mistrust and fear inside Paris.

The Jacobins Strike

Supported by the masses, especially the radical *sansculottes*, the Jacobins became the dominant force within the Convention. Because of the various threats to the revolution, the Jacobins were able to make the moderate Girondins look like enemies of the state.

Extreme elements operating outside the Convention, encouraged by the journalist Marat, began to press for the overthrow of the Girondins. After a series of mob demonstrations between 29 May and 2 June, the Girondins were expelled from the Convention. Many were imprisoned and later executed.

One Girondin supporter, Charlotte Corday, took her revenge on the man she considered to be most responsible

Below: *A Girondin supporter, Charlotte Corday, holds her dagger over Jean Paul Marat, who lies dead in his bath.*

Left: A female sans-culotte. The sans-culottes saw themselves as the protectors of the revolution. They were constantly on the look-out for evidence of counter-revolutionary activity, whether it was a badly termed phrase used in everyday conversation, or even a lack of enthusiasm shown for the new republic.

for the destruction of the Girondins. Arriving at Marat's house on 13 July 1793, she asked to see him saying she had important information about counter-revolutionary activities. Marat, suffering from a skin disease, was sitting in a high copper bath but, ever eager to root out counter-revolutionaries, he agreed to see her. Once in Marat's room, Corday pulled out a knife and plunged it into his heart, killing him instantly. Dropping the knife she said calmly, *'The deed is done; the monster is dead.'* Corday was tried and sent to the guillotine.

With the removal of the Girondins, the Jacobins were now able to dominate political life, as the French revolution entered its next and most ferocious phase.

CLUBS AND FACTIONS

While the revolutionaries were agreed that the old political system had to be transformed, they agreed on little else. Within the Convention – and its forerunner, the Assembly – various political groups or factions fought for power.

The most moderate of these factions, the Feuillants, had hoped to include the king within the political system, but they were swept aside as the revolution gained momentum. The Girondins – so called because many of their leaders came from the Gironde region of south-west France – believed in making a clean break with the past, but they in turn were usurped by the more radical Jacobins, led by Danton and Maximilien Robespierre.

The Jacobin Club – which took its name from the monastery of St. Jacob where its members met – operated within the Convention, but it also organized and encouraged the masses outside to take direct and often violent action. In this way, the Jacobins were able to undermine the authority of the Convention, and took overall power in June 1793.

A meeting of the Jacobin Club. The Jacobins favoured an extreme course for the revolution.

THE JACOBIN DICTATORSHIP

By July of 1793, the Jacobins and other radical revolutionaries had succeeded in ousting the moderates from the government. Within the Convention, power was concentrated into two small groups, the Committee for General Security and the Committee of Public Safety. Whoever had control of these committees had control of the revolution, and the Convention itself declined in importance and power.

A key figure in the Committee of Public Safety was the enigmatic and calculating Maximilien Robespierre. He gathered around him a band of devoted followers, notably the ruthless Georges Couthon, and Louis de Saint-Just, whose cold, heartless manner earned him the title, the 'Angel of Death'.

Right and below: *As the revolution became increasingly savage, the guillotine proved too slow to keep up with the killings. Outside Paris, faster methods of execution had to be found.*
In Lyons (right), 300 federalists were blasted to bits by cannon fire.
In Nantes (below), 2,000 victims were taken out in barges to the estuary of the river Loire, where they were stripped naked, bound in pairs and thrown into the water to drown.

While Robespierre plotted to gain control of the Committee of Public Safety, the revolution became ever more savage. This was the time of the Terror, which meant government through violence and fear. The Terror was a deliberate policy adopted by the Jacobins to eliminate all opposition. At any time of the day or night, a body of armed men carrying a warrant from the Committee of Public Safety could turn up outside a suspect's house. They would drag the suspect from his or her home to prison, then to trial and probable execution.

The Terror at Work

During the autumn of 1793, the disgraced Girondins were tried and executed, as was the former queen, Marie Antoinette. The guillotine hardly rested, and the fear generated by the Terror gained momentum. In one of his many attacks upon the so-called traitors to the revolution, Saint-Just declared: *'A man is guilty of a crime against the Republic when he takes pity on prisoners. He is guilty because he has no desire for virtue. He is guilty because he is opposed to the Terror.'* [10] In this atmosphere, a simple denunciation by a spiteful neighbour was enough to send a person to the guillotine; many personal scores were settled in this way.

TIMELINE

1793
27 July: Robespierre joins Couthon and Saint-Just on the powerful Committee of Public Safety.
23 August: Decree of the *levée en masse* (universal military service).
5 September: Terror is declared 'the order of the day'.
16 October: Execution of Marie Antoinette.
24-31 October: Trial and execution of Girondin leaders.

1794
14-24 March: Arrest, trial and execution of Hébertists.
30 March-5 April: Arrest, trial and execution of Danton and his supporters.
8 June: Festival of the Supreme Being.
26 June: French victory at the battle of Fleurus leads to the reconquest of Belgium.
27 July: Denunciation of Robespierre in the Convention.
28 July: Execution of Robespierre and his followers.

Je suis le véritable Père Duchesne; foutre!

LA PLUS GRANDE
DE TOUTES LES JOIES
DU
PERÉ DUCHESNE.
APRES avoir vu, de ses propres yeux, la tête

Above: *The title page of Hébert's journal,* Le Père Duchesne; *its name was taken from a popular theatrical figure. The paper was a vehicle for expressing the Hébertists' extremist views.*

At the end of 1793, the French army gained a series of victories which ensured that the threat of foreign invasion was over for good. Within France, the many revolts and internal disputes had either been suppressed or died down. Thus, for the first time, the Jacobin revolution was safe from attack. However, this new situation was to cause its own problems. Previously, threats to the revolution had forced the Jacobins to act together. Now, this unity began to break down, and opposing factions emerged.

On one side were the extremists led by the newspaper editor Jacques René Hébert (1757-94). This group, known as the Hébertists, wanted to increase the activities of the Terror. Opposing them were the Indulgents, led by Danton and the journalist Camille Desmoulins, who argued for a relaxation of the Terror. Standing outside this conflict was Robespierre. Robespierre's personal dislike for Hébert and Danton was combined with an ambition to bring the increasingly wayward revolution under his sole control. A cunning politician, Robespierre set about isolating the Hébertists and the Indulgents.

MAXIMILIEN ROBESPIERRE (1758-94)

A lawyer in Arras when the revolution began, Maximilien Robespierre was elected to the National Assembly in 1789, where he proved to be a hard-working deputy and a sound organizer. Lacking the flamboyance of men such as Mirabeau and Danton, Robespierre drew on his skill as a politician. He gathered around him a close-knit band of loyal supporters who worked themselves into positions of power within the revolutionary government.

Robespierre was described by Marat as the 'incorruptible', a name which stuck because of his honesty and inflexibility in personal and political matters. He became obsessed with the need for virtue in government and, in order to impose his moral attitude on the revolution, he eliminated all who stood in his way. In the end, Robespierre's virtue was not able to save him from the guillotine. Robespierre was a stern man who rose to the top through his energy and dedication to the revolution but who aroused no feelings of warmth from his comrades.

Maximilien Robespierre, the last and most extreme of the Jacobin leaders. After getting rid of Danton, Robespierre became the undisputed master of the revolution.

A PLEA FOR TOLERANCE

Camille Desmoulins was one of Danton's leading associates. In an attack on the Hébertists he argued for an end to the violent cruelty of the Terror: *'Do you want to exterminate all your enemies by the guillotine? But this would be the greatest folly. Can you destroy one on the scaffold without making ten enemies from among his family and friends? Do you really believe that it is women, old men, the feeble who are dangerous? Of your true enemies only the cowards and sick are left. . .'* [11]

Left: *A revolutionary tribunal at work. A family (on the left) has been brought forward to answer charges of counter-revolutionary activity. In these affairs, justice was often a matter of hit or miss and the innocent were regularly sent to their deaths.*

The Hébertists were the first to be destroyed. Robespierre used the hostility of the Indulgents towards the Hébertists, and accused several of Hébert's leading supporters of being involved in foreign plots to overthrow the Convention. On 14 March 1794, the Committee of Public Safety arrested Hébert and eighteen of his supporters, and within ten days they had been tried and sent to the guillotine.

The Death of Danton

Danton's central role in the revolution and his popularity with the people made him more difficult to eliminate. However, under the guiding hand of Saint-Just, charges of corruption were drawn up against Danton and his supporters. Danton had enjoyed the pleasures of his position. Once he had boasted: *'Delicious food, splendid liquor, women of one's dreams – that's what power wins when you grab it.'*[12] The charges did not add up to much, but suitably dressed up by Saint-Just they were sufficient for an arrest warrant to be issued against Danton and his followers.

On 30 March, the Dantonists were swiftly arrested. At his trial, Danton's voice boomed out across the courtroom, and his powerful defence began to unnerve the prosecution. Fearing a possible uprising to save Danton, the trial was hurriedly cut short and a sentence of death was passed on Danton and those who stood trial alongside him.

Danton went to the guillotine defiant to the last, making jokes and encouraging his supporters in their final minutes. Before going under the blade he said to the executioner: *'Above all, don't forget to show my head to the people. It's well worth having a look at.'*[13]

Above: *Louis de Saint-Just, Robespierre's loyal supporter and the ruthless enemy of Danton.*

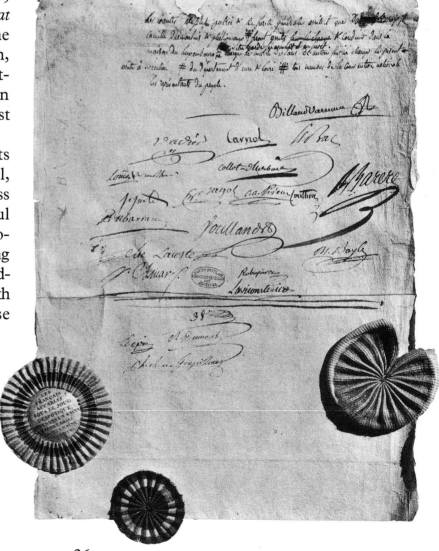

THE HUMANE KILLING MACHINE

Despite its grisly image, the guillotine was deliberately designed as a means of executing criminals more quickly and less painfully. Whereas an axe could take several attempts to remove the head, the guillotine did its work with one swift blow.

The machine was named after its designer, a doctor called Joseph Ignace Guillotin (1738-1814). A deputy in the National Assembly, Dr Guillotin had proposed the machine in December 1789, although it was not until April 1792 that an early version was used in a public execution. Almost immediately, the guillotine became the preferred means of execution and claimed thousands of lives during the French Revolution.

The guillotine hard at work during a session of executions conducted on 13 August 1792.

The Triumph of Virtue

Left: *The warrant for the arrest of Danton and his followers. Robespierre's small, neat signature can be seen near the centre.*

Robespierre was now free to direct the revolution on what he believed was a 'virtuous' course. Having got rid of so many old religious and social customs, Robespierre encouraged the development of a new moral code.

The new moral code was considered better suited to the aims and beliefs of revolutionary France. In effect, it was to be an alternative 'civil religion', stressing individual virtue, where the old Christian god was replaced by a new god of nature and reason.

In the political field, Robespierre imposed his authority on the revolution. Along with other radical Jacobins, he had once relied heavily on direct action from the *sans-culotte* masses in the struggle for power. Now that power had been achieved, he no longer needed them. Troubled also by their unruly behaviour, he set about removing their influence on government. Many of the *sans-culotte* leaders were imprisoned or executed.

Ironically, however, Robespierre and his associates were thus isolating themselves from popular support; their power was based on terror alone. Other members of the Convention resented Robespierre's autocratic powers and, fearful for their own safety, they looked for an opportunity to unseat him.

A vast ceremony, called The Festival of the Supreme Being, was held in Paris on 8 June 1794 as a public celebration of the new religion of virtue.

A NEW CALENDAR

As part of the movement to get rid of old Christian symbols, the Jacobin revolutionaries developed a new calendar in October 1793. The year began on 22 September (the date of the declaration of the French Republic in 1792) and was divided into twelve months. Each month was thirty days long and was divided into three ten-day weeks (the remaining five days of the year were set aside for national holidays).

An illustration from the new revolutionary calendar shows the month of Pluviôse, the season of rains.

Vendémiaire	Vintage	22 September-21 October
Brumaire	Mists	22 October-20 November
Frimaire	Frosts	21 November-20 December
Nivôse	Snow	21 December-19 January
Pluviôse	Rains	20 January-18 February
Ventôse	Winds	19 February-20 March
Germinal	Buds	21 March-19 April
Floréal	Flowers	20 April-19 May
Prairial	Meadows	20 May-18 June
Messidor	Harvest	19 June-18 July
Thermidor	Sun	19 July-17 August
Fructidor	Fruits	18 August-16 September

Left: *The arrest of Robespierre and his allies on 9 Thermidor. Robespierre is lying on the table, having tried to kill himself to prevent the humiliation of arrest, trial and public execution.*
The attempt failed, however; Robespierre only succeeded in blowing away his lower jaw.
The bandage around his neck and jaw is visible in this illustration.

The Convention got its chance on 26 July 1794 when Robespierre grandly attacked a number of Convention members during a debate. To his surprise, the men were vigorously defended by other members. Criticism of Robespierre's rule spread outside the Convention on to the streets of Paris. This sudden upsurge of opposition grew swiftly. The next day, a confident Convention voted for the arrest of Robespierre, knowing that the *sans-culotte* masses would not come to his aid. Robespierre and his followers were seized, in an event known by its revolutionary calendar name of 9 Thermidor. They were tried and sent to the guillotine. In the space of only two days, the Jacobin dictatorship had been overthrown.

THE REVOLUTION RESTRAINED

After the fall of Robespierre, the Convention – led by moderates – quickly reasserted its authority over the Committee of Public Safety. The Jacobin Club was closed; its leaders were thrown into prison and many were executed. In the provinces, those who had suffered at the hands of the Jacobins took their revenge. In the south of France, the wave of anti-Jacobin violence that followed came to be called the White Terror.

The Convention had to face renewed unrest within France. The severe winter of 1794-5 and a bad harvest caused widespread hardship, and in Paris there were

Below: The closure of the Jacobin Club on 12 November 1794 confirmed the end of the radicals' domination of the revolution. From now on, the revolution would adopt a more moderate tone, yet many of those who had supported Robespierre would fear for their lives.

PARIS AFTER THE JACOBINS

Following the downfall of Robespierre, the feared hand of the Terror was lifted. The enormous sense of relief felt by large numbers of the people of Paris is evident in this account by M. Thibadeau: *'Immediately after 9 Thermidor, all hearts embraced the most joyful hopes. It was affecting to witness the zest of citizens searching for each other, exchanging their experiences, good or bad, of the Terror, congratulating or comforting. Jacks in office no longer looked stern or threatening, only showed minor malice or shame. Some, through cowardice, or indeed sincerity, even took part in the general rejoicings. Among victims, calm happiness had replaced inhibition and wretchedness. It was a sort of resurrection of the dead . . .'* [14]

Right: During a sans-culotte demonstration against the Convention on 20 May 1795 (1 Prairial) a deputy called Jean Féraud was killed. This painting shows the mob taunting the Convention president with Féraud's severed head.

TIMELINE

1794
30-31 July:
Reorganization of the
Committee of Public
Safety.
12 November: Closure
of the Jacobin Club.

1795
1 April: (12 Germinal)
An uprising of *sans-
culottes* is suppressed.
May-June: Worst
excesses of the White
Terror occur.

1799
9-10 November:
Bonaparte seizes power
in the *coup d'état* of
18-19 Brumaire.

repeated demonstrations from the poor demanding bread. Fearful that such outbursts might lead to a re-emergence of the Jacobin-supporting *sans-culottes*, the Convention brought in the French army to crush street protests.

The Rule of Five

Election to the Convention was restricted to the better-off, property-owning classes, in order to prevent the masses from having any chance of gaining power. Within the Convention, control was handed over to a group of five individuals known as the Directory. These men were the effective rulers of France, and would remain so until November 1799.

Throughout the latter half of the 1790s, the Directory tried to put the country back on a more secure economic footing. Fortunately for them, harvests improved and the Republic's financial problems were reduced. Yet the Directory was forced to tread a difficult line between the two forces that wanted its downfall. On the one hand were the remains of the Jacobin *sans-culottes* and, on the other, the royalists. To balance these, the Directory relied increasingly on the army to ensure order in the country.

The Army Ascendant

After an uncertain start, the French army had prospered during the revolution. A string of victories over Prussia, Austria, Holland and Britain had forged the army into a highly professional force, the best in Europe. Its leading commanders were men who had risen through the ranks, and who had formed a keen sense of the importance of politics in the development of their careers. Of these, the most successful was Napoleon Bonaparte, a soldier who had thrown the Austrians out of Italy.

Above: *By the time of the Consulate, the wealthier members of French society began to adopt a more elegant lifestyle.*

General Bonaparte was a man whose ambitions extended beyond victory on the field of battle; his eyes were firmly set on gaining supreme power over France, then Europe. On 9-10 November 1799, Bonaparte overthrew the Directory and, backed by his troops, effectively seized control of the country. The new form of government was known as the Consulate, and was led by three consuls: Emmanuel Joseph Sieyès (1748-1836), Roger Ducos (1754-1816) and Bonaparte. Only Bonaparte, supported by military force, held real power. The new military dictatorship brought the French Revolution to a close. In 1804, Bonaparte crowned himself Emperor of the French.

Having defended France from external attack, the French armies went on to the offensive and conquered large areas of western Europe. The most successful of the new generation of French commanders was Napoleon Bonaparte, who won many battles fighting the Austrians in Italy.

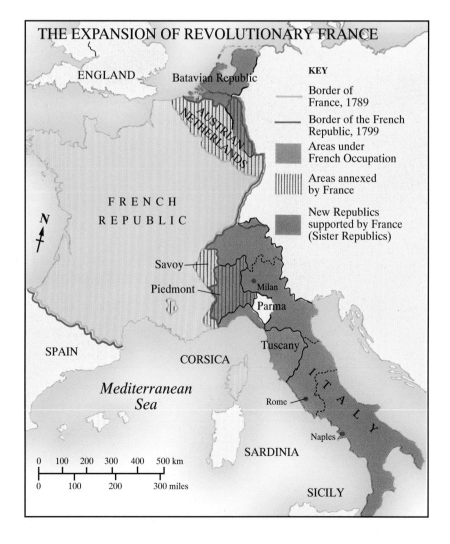

THE EXPANSION OF REVOLUTIONARY FRANCE

ENGLAND

Batavian Republic

AUSTRIAN NETHERLANDS

FRENCH REPUBLIC

N

Savoy

Piedmont

Milan

Parma

SPAIN

CORSICA

Tuscany

Mediterranean Sea

Rome

ITALY

SARDINIA

Naples

SICILY

KEY

—— Border of France, 1789

—— Border of the French Republic, 1799

Areas under French Occupation

||| Areas annexed by France

New Republics supported by France (Sister Republics)

0 100 200 300 400 500 km

0   100   200   300 miles

NAPOLEON BONAPARTE (1769-1821)

The son of a poor, minor landowner in Corsica, Bonaparte entered the French army as a junior officer in the artillery. At the outbreak of revolution he became an enthusiastic supporter of the radical cause, and won fame for his recapture of Toulon from the British-aided royalists. Supported initially by Robespierre and later by Barras (a key figure in the Directory) Bonaparte's rise was rapid. In 1796 (at the age of 27) he was given command of the French Army of Italy, and in a brilliant eighteen-month campaign he defeated the Austrians and brought Italy under French control.

With the help of his supporters, Bonaparte seized power over France in the coup of 18 Brumaire (9-10 November 1799). He proved himself to be a highly capable administrator as well as a great soldier: a new legal code was established (called the *Code Napoléon*), local government was reorganized and new roads were built.

After his coronation in 1804, Napoleon began a series of successful military campaigns which made him virtual master of Europe. Eventually, however, his ambition brought about his downfall, as the countries of Europe banded together to get rid of him. In 1812 he suffered his first major setback when he invaded Russia, and was finally defeated by an Anglo-Prussian army at the Battle of Waterloo in 1815. He spent the rest of his life in exile on the tiny island of St. Helena in the South Atlantic Ocean.

In 1804, Napoleon crowned himself Emperor of the French and established himself as the supreme power over much of Europe.

THE FRENCH REVOLUTION AND THE OUTSIDE WORLD

The French Revolution was one of the great turning points of history. At the time, people were aware that important and lasting changes were taking place and, since then, historians have argued over its causes and consequences. Although England had experienced enormous political and social upheaval in the seventeenth century and the American colonists had set up a new political system after the War of Independence, it was the French Revolution that transformed the way peoples throughout the world thought they should be governed.

The violence of the revolution is often emphasized over other more significant factors. The brutal deaths of 35,000-40,000 people during this period cannot easily be glossed over but, compared with the destruction encountered in a

As many as 1,200 people may have been killed during the September Massacres of 1792. It was scenes like this that gave the French Revolution its reputation for violent ferocity.

A statue of Louis XVI is pulled down to the cheers of the crowd on 13 August 1792. The position of European monarchs would never be completely secure again.

major Napoleonic battle, for example, such figures need to be put into perspective: at Waterloo, French casualties alone exceeded 40,000 men in a single day's fighting.

When Napoleon was defeated in 1815, the countries of Europe tried to turn the clock back to 1789. The old French royal family was returned to the throne, but Louis XVIII (the brother of the executed Louis XVI) was reluctantly forced to accept that the world had changed. The central consequence of the revolution was that it had created a new political culture where people were equal under the law. The old order of privilege, based on noble birth, was never to return. Instead, anyone – at least in theory – could find a way to the top. Monarchs who failed to realize this fact did not last long.

A Revolutionary Future

The French Revolution has been seen as a middle-class uprising, in which those with money and property gained the greatest advantages. This is largely true but, through the example of the Jacobin *sans-culottes*, the oppressed poor had been given a vision of what was possible if the people rose up to take direct action. This possibility played an important part in the development of socialism, the political system that lay behind so many of the revolutions of the nineteenth and twentieth centuries. It may be argued that the central importance of the French Revolution lay in the way that it acted as a model for future revolution.

A political cartoon showing the 'awakening' of the Third Estate to the dismay of the nobility and clergy. From 1789 onwards, the common people would play an increasingly important role in political life.

GLOSSARY

Alliance Countries or states working together.

Ancien régime The political and social system in France before the revolution under which royalty, the nobility and the clergy enjoyed great privileges over the people (see also feudal system).

Artillery A branch of the army that is trained to use large guns.

Autocratic The use of total power by one person.

Bankruptcy Having no money.

Clergy The people who carry out the religious duties of the Christian Churches.

Counter-revolutionaries People working against a revolution.

Coup d'état Seizing control of a country in a way that is not supported by the law.

Decree To state that something is law.

Depression A long period of economic difficulty, when trade and industry are weak.

Despotism A hard and strict absolute rule.

Divine right (to rule) The power to rule that was said to be given by God.

Economic (situation) The wealth of a country.

Émigrés People who leave their own country to live in another country, especially for political reasons.

Extremist A person with strong views that are very different to the views held by most people.

Faction A small group within a larger political group with which it disagrees.

Federalist A person who supports a federal system of government. Under this system, a country is divided into a number of areas which handle many of their own affairs independently of the rest of the country.

Feudal system A social system under which royalty and the nobility have rights and power over the majority of the people.

Manifesto A written, public statement of intentions made by, for example, a head of state or government.

Military dictatorship Absolute rule by the military.

Militia An army put together from the civilian population.

Moderate (revolutionary) A person who understands the need for major change but who wants to keep some things as they are.

Orator A person who is skilled at making public speeches.

Oratory The art of speaking in public.

Patriot A person who is loyal to his or her country.

Prussia The most important of the group of states that became unified as Germany in 1871.

Radical An extreme political view or a person who holds such a view.

Republic A state that is governed by the people or their elected representatives, not by a king or queen.

Royalist A person who supports the idea of having a king or queen at the head of a country.

Sans-culottes From the French words meaning 'without breeches', breeches being short trousers fastened at the knee and worn by the nobility and the wealthy in the eighteenth century. The poor, on the other hand, wore trousers, so *sans-culottes* became the name for the revolutionaries.

Socialism A political theory in which every member of a community is involved in the ownership and control of manufacture and trade.

Tax A charge made by the state on an individual's wealth, whether on money or property. Taxes are collected by the state and used as the state thinks best.

Vintage The time of year when grapes are harvested for making wine.

Watch Either the collective name for guards patrolling the streets to keep the peace, especially at night, or the period of time when a guard is on duty.

FURTHER INFORMATION

BOOKS

The Fall of the Bastille by Nathaniel Harris
    (Dryad Press, 1986)
The French Revolution by Hervé Luxardo (trans. Nan
    Buranelli) (Hamish Hamilton Children's Books, 1989)
The French Revolution by Peter Mantin
    (Heinemann Educational, 1992)
The French Revolution by Margaret Mulvihill
    (Franklin Watts, 1989)
The French Revolution and Napoleon by Stephen Pratt
    (Wayland, 1992)

For older readers

A History of Modern France: Volume 1 1715-1799 by Alfred
    Cobban (Penguin Books, 1990)
The French Revolution by Christopher Hibbert
    (Penguin Books, 1982)
A Concise History of France by Roger Price
    (Cambridge University Press, 1993)
The French Revolution by J. M. Roberts
    (Oxford University Press, 1978)
Citizens: A Chronicle of the French Revolution by Simon
    Schama (Viking, 1989)
Voices of the Revolution by Peter Vansittart (Collins, 1989,
    now out of print but may be available from libraries)

Fiction

A Tale of Two Cities by Charles Dickens (there are a
    number of editions available)
A Place of Greater Safety by Hilary Mantel (Penguin, 1993)

FILMS

Danton directed by Andrzej Wajda, 1982, with Gerard
    Depardieu as Danton.
The Scarlet Pimpernel directed by Harold Young, 1934,
    with Leslie Howard and Merle Oberon. The politics of
    the Revolution are pushed into the background of this
    story of romance and adventure.

SOURCES OF QUOTES

1 Quoted by Simon Schama in *Citizens: A Chronicle of the French Revolution* (Viking, 1989).
2 Quoted by Christopher Hibbert in *The French Revolution* (Penguin Books, 1982).
3 Quoted by Peter Vansittart in *Voices of the Revolution* (Collins, 1989).
4 Quoted by Simon Schama in *Citizens*.
5 Quoted by Peter Vansittart in *Voices of the Revolution*.
6 As above.
7 Quoted by Christopher Hibbert in *The French Revolution*.
8 As above.
9 As above.
10 As above.
11 Quoted by Peter Vansittart in *Voices of the Revolution*.
12 Quoted by Simon Schama in *Citizens*.
13 As above.
14 Quoted by Peter Vansittart in *Voices of the Revolution*.

INDEX